I Am Beautiful

A Multicultural Mosaic

by

Nneka Edwards

I Am Beautiful! A Multicultural Mosaic
©2017 by Nneka Edwards
All rights reserved

Designed by Nneka Edwards

Published by Nneka Edwards, Trinidad and Tobago
Second edition

ISBN: 978-976-95855-7-7

Printed in the United States

About the Book

"I Am Beautiful!" is a multicultural-mosaic representation of the word beautiful. Through this multi-ethnic poetry-collage, travel the world from continent to continent, and culture to culture, to see and appreciate the work of art which each one of us truly is. Twenty young ladies are painted from a rich palette of cultural motifs unique to the people-group being portrayed. The lovely paper-collage illustrations represent the rainbow spectrum of global diversity. The colourful depictions will make it fun for you to test your world knowledge by seeing if you can determine the national or ethnic identity of each character. The country and continent guide at the back of the book confirms answers. While only a few countries or regions were selected, this book is designed to paint a warm kaleidoscopic picture of our global village.

I am beautiful ...

... and I see beauty

I am Coco-Mo.
My face is sprinkled
with cinnamon freckles.
With my almond hazelnut eyes
and mochaccino skin,
I'm a sun-kissed kaiso thing.

I am Valley of Flowers.
My spirit is wild and free.
With my eagle eyes
and feathers in my hair,
I'm a beautiful prayer.

I am Milk-Lily.
I have strawberry waves
and fruity freckles.
With my green-gem eyes
and plum-button nose,
I'm a budding rose.

I am Snowflake Daughter.
I have rosebud cheeks
and grey-wolf eyes.
With my warm coat
ringed with snowy fur,
I'm a pink-ice girl.

I am Cha-Cha Chica.
My feet fiesta
and my soul sweetly siestas.
With hummingbird song
dancing in my black-bean eyes,
I'm a piñata surprise.

I am Bossa Nova.
Samba sways my step
as tamborim drums call.
With my chocolate-fudge cheeks
and caramel-mocha tone,
I'm a precious stone.

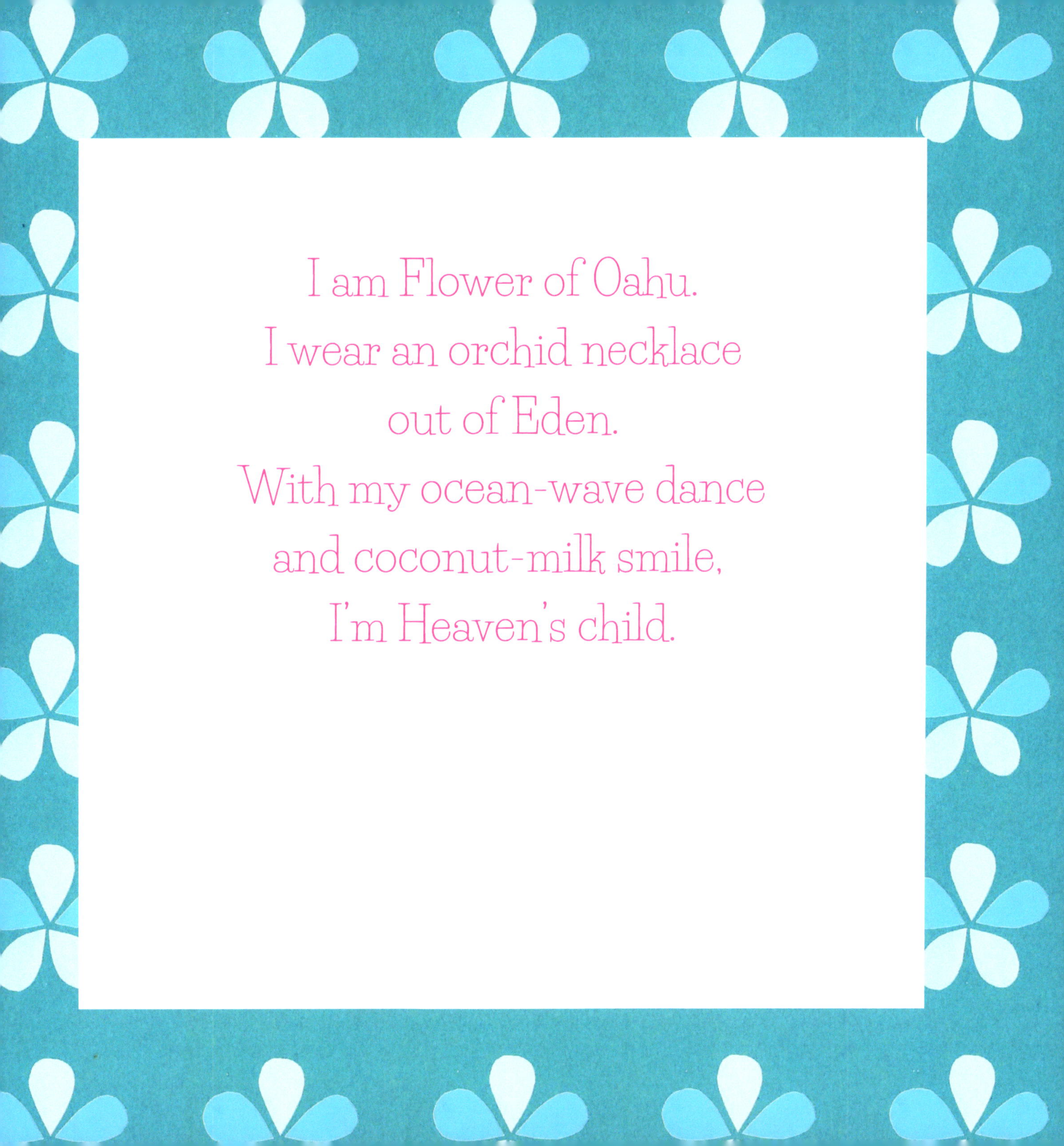

I am Flower of Oahu.
I wear an orchid necklace
out of Eden.
With my ocean-wave dance
and coconut-milk smile,
I'm Heaven's child.

I am Jannali Moon.
I have bronze-river hair
and soft koala eyes.
With tribal patterns
crossing my finely crafted nose,
I'm rock art painting prose.

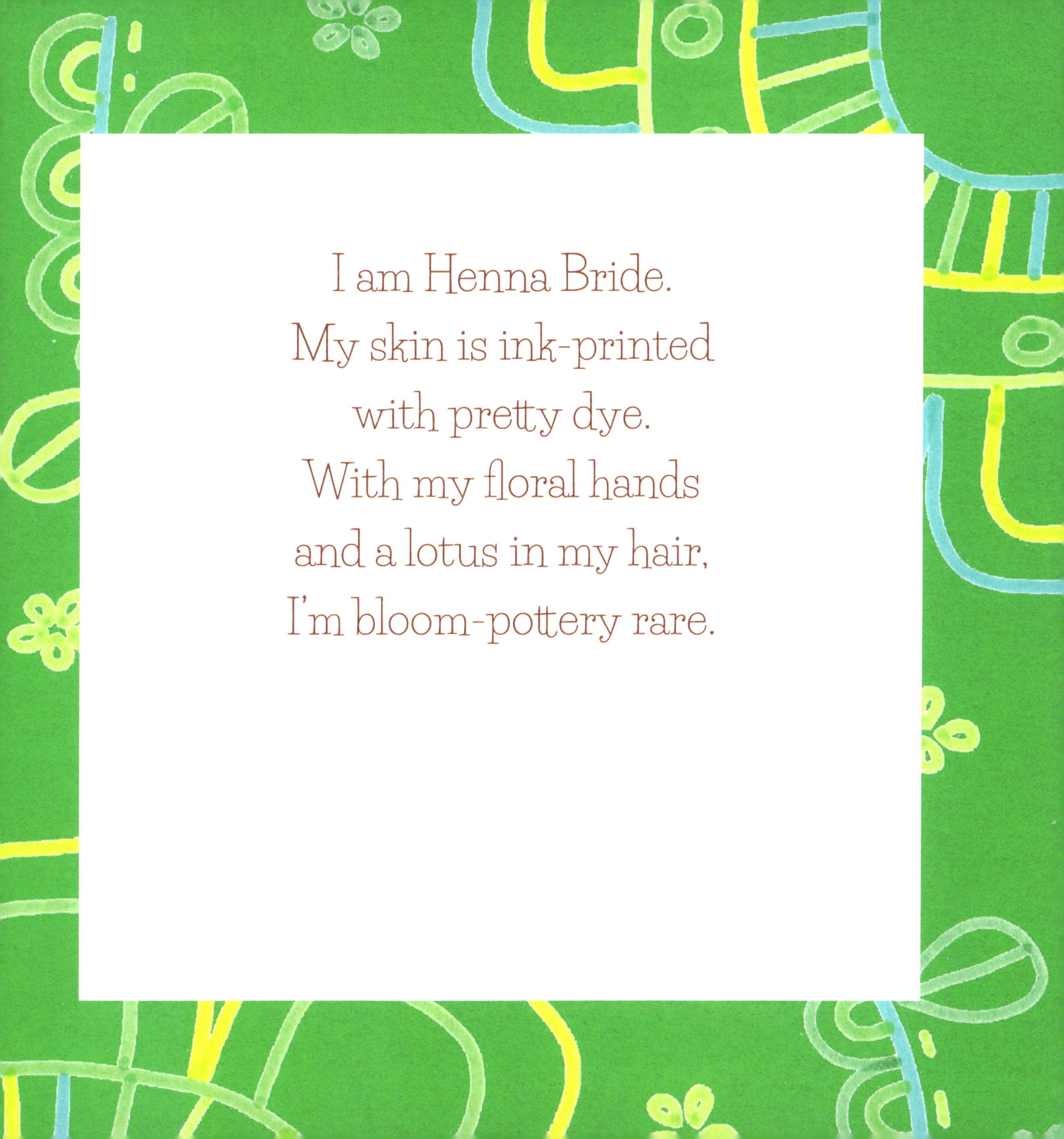

I am Henna Bride.
My skin is ink-printed
with pretty dye.
With my floral hands
and a lotus in my hair,
I'm bloom-pottery rare.

I Am Asoka Jewel.
I have a java-coffee
peanut-sweet tan.
With my ginger-tea soul
and dye-print sarong dress,
I'm a true princess.

I am Pink Plum Blossom.
I wear porcelain chopsticks
in my hair.
With my melon-seed eyes
and rose-blush cheeks,
I'm an empress peach.

I am Morning Calm.
I have pomegranate cheeks
and dawn in my smile.
With my princess gown
and fan-spreading dance,
I'm oriental romance.

I am Water-Lily Hana.
A cherry-blossom smile
bridges my lotus cheeks.
Wrapped in springtime silk
with a pink-sash bow,
I'm a gift aglow.

I am Sunshine Dawning.
My barley-gold tress
matches my scarf.
With raspberry cheeks glowing
as snow gently falls,
I'm a painted doll.

I am Bohemian.
My green-diamond eyes
match my flowery frills.
With my caravan soul
on a quest to touch the dawn,
I'm an epic song.

I am Noémie.
My eyes sparkle
with bubbly champagne joy.
With my oh-là-là à la mode style
and flowery perfume,
I'm a garden bloom.

I am Lyrical Laurel.
My eyes are set like copper-tone crystal
in olive skin.
With a lyre strumming my soul
and a flower in my hair,
I'm sweet folksong cheer.

I am Young-Maiden Maasai.
I am robed in rainbow prints
that promise joy.
With my shaved head
and bands of colour circling my neck,
I'm a dark belle bedecked.

I am Mother of the Earth.
I pound yam in song
that flows like sweet palm wine.
With a queenly wrap
crowning pretty prints, as I rejoice,
I'm a deep-soul voice.

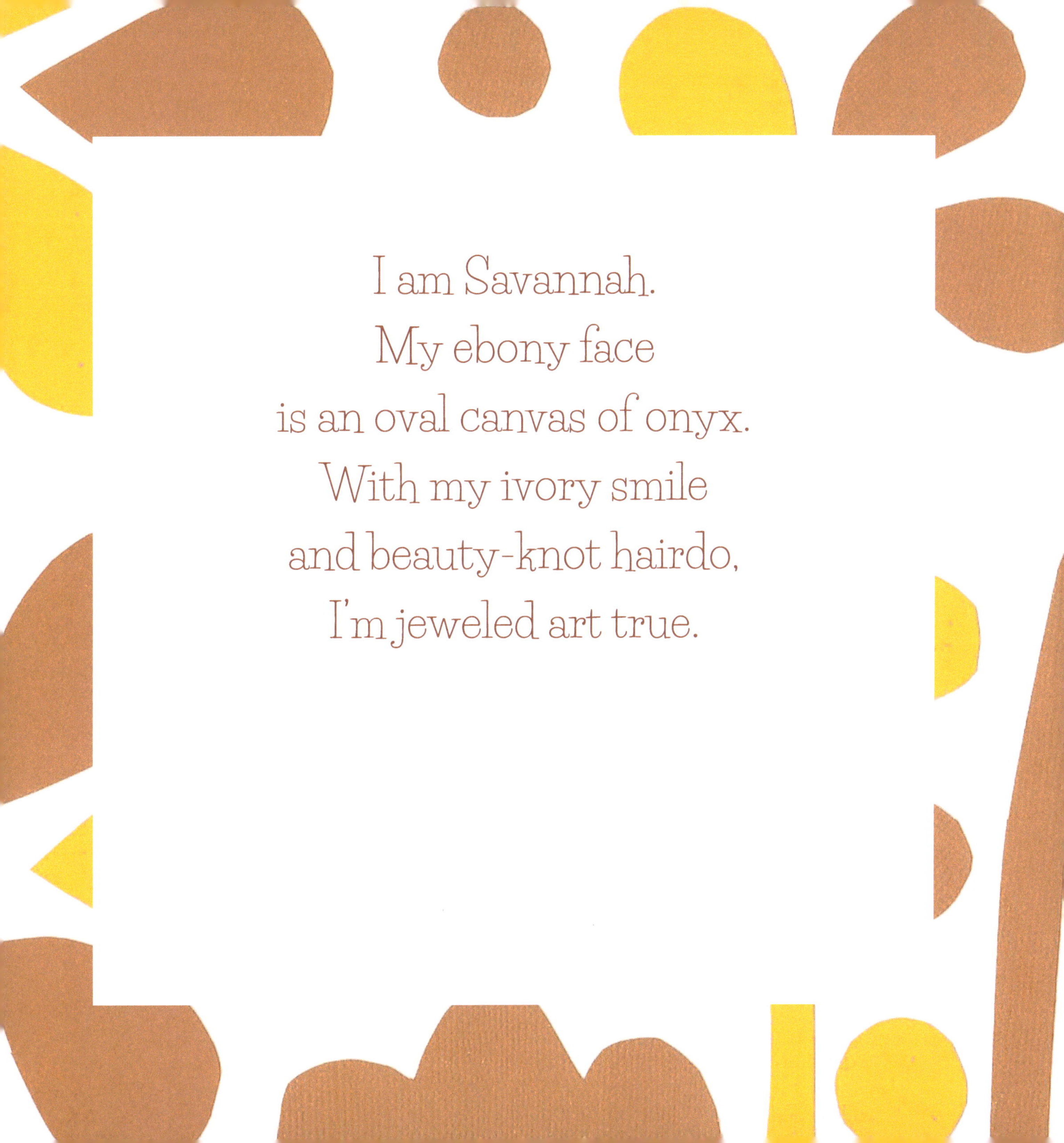
I am Savannah.
My ebony face
is an oval canvas of onyx.
With my ivory smile
and beauty-knot hairdo,
I'm jeweled art true.

I am beautiful ...

... and I see beauty

List of Continents
Asia
Africa
Europe
Australasia
North America
South America

Cultures, Regions, Countries and Ethnic Groups
1. Caribbean
2. United States (Native American)
3. North America (or Ireland)
4. Canada (Inuit)
5. Latin America
6. Brazil
7. Hawaii
8. Australia (Aboriginal person)
9. Indonesia
10. India
11. China
12. Korea
13. Japan
14. Russia
15. Romani Traveller
16. France
17. Greece
18. Kenya (Maasai)
19. Nigeria
20. Africa

About the Author

Nneka Edwards is a Caribbean poet and author who hails from Trinidad and Tobago in the southern Caribbean. Nneka speaks Spanish, French, Chinese and knows some German, Korean, Japanese and Portuguese. She holds a bachelor's degree in East Asian Studies and a master's degree in International Cooperation.